NEXT
X
20

NEXT 20

A FORMULA FOR CREATING A MORE PERFECT UNION

CLAUDIA JAMES

JAKATA HOUSE

NEXT20: A Formula for Creating a More Perfect Union

JAKATA
HOUSE

Published by Jakata House
Denver, CO

JAMES, CLAUDIA, Author
NEXT20
CLAUDIA JAMES

ISBN: 978-0-692-94040-2

POLITICAL SCIENCE / Commentary & Opinion
POLITICAL SCIENCE / Political Process / Political Advocacy

QUANTITY PURCHASES: Schools, companies, professional
groups, clubs, and other organizations may qualify for special
terms when ordering quantities of this title. For information,
email next20now@gmail.com

To my sister Tanja Kubas-Meyer, who represents the many people who dedicate their life to advocacy in support of improved policies. Only because of them, and their tireless work, can a formula like NEXT20 be realized.

Travis, Kevin, and Julia,
it is your generation that is the most important.

CONTENTS

WHY NOW? ☆

OUR COUNTRY HAS BEEN OPERATING with the perception that by flip-flopping two parties back and forth, our goals will become "fair." As the years have gone by, this back and forth between two extremes has created *reaction*, not *action*. *Fair* is no longer a realistic or rational goal.

Consider this: What does anyone find rational about two children yanking a candy bar back and forth out of each other's hands and expecting the other to understand why it should be only theirs? There's nothing fair about that. A responsible parent would say "split it in half and share it or you will lose it all together." What is fair, healthy, and rational is *compromise*. Today we find our government and our people in a constant struggle for the entire candy bar.

Our country can no longer deny that "political balance" in our nation has failed. The heart of America is suffering, down to its last few heartbeats, and there is nothing *fair* about that for anyone. The dire situation we find ourselves in today did not begin in November of 2016. It has been building for a long time, and unaddressed, we now find ourselves in an acute state. This failure is a sign that this is the moment to seize the opportunity to change how we operate. The only chance to save the heartbeat of our beloved country is through *compromise*. It has to happen now!

While searching for answers and seeking solutions, people are feeling more vulnerable and growing more desperate. They feel they are being taken advantage of by a system that does not recognize their needs. When people feel they have nothing to lose, there is a greater risk of violence. And, as reality unfolds before our country's eyes, we watch those who support the current administration polish their weapons in preparation to protect their newly found representation. Dual terror, homegrown and foreign, on our own soil and abroad, is where we are headed. Terror grows in countries that are broken. Terror thrives in countries burdened by oppression. Our country cannot afford to risk more division due to another flip of parties. The goal must not be to undermine the parties, but to utilize the benefits of the core ideologies that drive people to hold tightly to their party affiliations. NOW is the time for leadership to draw constructively from those ideologies and offer representation of compromise to the majority.

NOW is the time for leadership to draw constructively from those ideologies and offer representation of compromise to the majority.

Many groups—from the Independents who identify with both or neither party, to the non-voters, and to the 40% who actually vote—see the dangers of this tug-of-war system and are ready to stand behind multi-affiliation representation.

This country does not need a third party, it needs leadership that *unites* a common set of principles representing the majority. One that is dedicated to the goals of *all*.

The problems in our country stem from consistently experiencing loss no matter what party we choose. If we do not win because of the candidate we voted for, we then lose because we must pay the price for having won. Our limitations stem from the *spin* of what each party will not provide.

NEXT20 *offers the option to choose compromise over loss!*

While strategizing, our diverse needs, backgrounds and cultures must be taken into consideration. People do not want to have to choose between having a strong military or uplifting struggling communities. No one should be forced to choose between human rights or an

NEXT20 offers a new opportunity for our cultural ideologies to become relevant through the elimination of choice.

income tax break. And nobody should have to choose between affordable premiums or adequate health care. NEXT20 offers the solution of purpose over party. Most importantly, NEXT20 offers a new opportunity for our cultural ideologies to become relevant through the elimination of choice.

Imagine if for the first time in history we could reach voter participation of 75% with 60% by voting for a multi-affiliation platform. Every four years it would increase by the sheer nature of progress, and the younger generations would vote because they would finally have leadership that allows them peaceful evaluation of the country's needs. NEXT20 benefits our country by absorbing the strengths of multiple leadership platforms, eliminating the dangers of absolutists and ensuring inclusivity of those committed to the goals we've had all along. We need NEXT20 now.

OUR PARTIES
NEED EACH OTHER

▷ DEMOCRATS

WHEN LISTENING TO THE MEMBERS of the struggling class talk about their apprehensive view of the Democratic Party, it becomes clear that they feel the problems they face simply do not matter to the party. The most ironic thing about Democrats is that they are disconnected from the very people they claim to defend. If Democrats were communicating effectively, we would not have to wonder why those who need support the most are not voting for them. The reality is that too many Democrats do not vote at all. Some would say that it is "politically correct" to be a Democrat because they perceive it to be the party that "cares." But if the people in need are not experiencing that support, then it is all for naught. It becomes idle, meaningless chatter with no manifestation in reality.

Democrats are known to be eloquent speakers, but the tendency is to use broad exaggerations that doom their ability to put their goals into action. Instead of promising "Free Education", and "Medicaid for All", they would be better off becoming a bit humble and take some accountability in the failings of healthcare and education reform. These systems have lacked attention in properly serving the people for decades, but Democrats offer these promises as if the public should feel secure in them. The party that claims to want to advocate for social systems should be relentless in proving those policies are worthy and consistent ones in which to invest. Suggesting that the wealthiest 2% will pay for it all is not only off-putting to the wealthy, but also does a disservice to everyone who deserves an honest and realistic plan. These are important topics and worthy of pragmatic execution, but Democratic candidates need to learn how to communicate to the public in an effective way. Democratic leaders have lost track of the main issues that separated them from Republicans in the last fifty years. The vast majority of constituents feel abandoned, and support of "the little guy" has no bearing in most people's realities.

The excuse that Democrats have not been able to accomplish more as a result of a Republican push back is only partially true. Not only do their social programs need to improve in efficiency, but the communities that are not being served must also be acknowledged. Our wealthiest and most progressive cities, many of which should be the example of a "liberal city," alienate their lower income communities with overwhelming costs of living, unaffordable housing, struggling schools and criminal injustices. Sadly, our best examples are poor examples.

The abilities and the strength of Democratic leaders are in question. The reason is that they hesitate to implement legislation. Even with strong conviction, the Democrats failed to fight hard enough to secure their desired Supreme Court Justice. Perhaps due to their dependence on big money donors, combatting Citizens United and campaign finance reform became a lesser priority. History also shows lost opportunities in securing policies that support national gun safety measures. The Democratic Party is also guilty of lack of compromise, not only with Republicans but also within their own party. Over the years, Democrats have relinquished their roles on the local level, creating even more vulnerability with imbalanced legislation. Lost opportunities for progress are clear as we have witnessed egomania override the interests of the greater good. The party that claims tolerance can be intolerant of legitimate policies, when those policies are not theirs.

Our country deserves thoughtful leadership, but one with a backbone to follow through.

The progressive goals of the Democratic Party are extremely important. For decades, this country has been waiting to reap the benefits of solid lasting policies that create an effective social support system, and environmental protections. The Democrats can achieve these vital measures through effective communication, embracing the skills of the Republican Party, and multi-affiliation compromise.

▶ REPUBLICANS

When watching the array of presidential candidates all representing the Republican Party in the last presidential election, it
is difficult to conceive of them as one party.

The Republican Party is, in actuality, at least four incohesive
groups: four separate groups operating and voting as one, for
the most part.

1. Mainstream Republicans are fiscally conservative and
   socially conscious, their voices are among the silenced in
   their party, and are likely to become Independents.
2. Libertarian Republicans seem to want all to be responsible,
   just for themselves, without evidence on how donations
   alone will sustain infrastructure and the most vulnerable.
3. Ultra Conservative Republicans whose agenda trends against
   the separation of church and state, while preaching consti-
   tutionality only when it does not go against their own views.
4. Nationalist Republicans, who we find primarily in the current administration, who think the U.S.A. comes first in all
   situations, even at the expense of their own people's diverse
   needs, and vastly ignore the fact that our country represents
   global leadership.

This is a big problem for Republicans, as it is confusing for the
party base to decipher. Honestly, it is confusing for everyone
to decipher. Over and over again, the Republican Party pres-
ents qualified presidential candidates and then tacks on an
Ultra Conservative VP candidate. As a result of choosing an

alliance to the extremists who turn a blind eye to greed and racism, mainstream Republicans lose their appeal to the majority, thereby losing their voice.

Ironically, the party that claims to be skilled at fiscal policy leads in states that suffer the highest levels of poverty. This is an unfortunate result of what could have been great examples.

The Ultra Conservatives and Nationalists are insignificant on their own and survive on the coattails of the Republican Party. Their claims of being the "party of values", the Party of "family values" and "Pro Life" has done more harm to them and the people, than good. Not only is it inappropriate for leadership to foist their ideals onto others' lives, but it falls on deaf ears when those values do not seem to apply in their own lives. Defunding care for women and children and cuts to Social Security and Medicare, without alternative support systems in place, is a far cry from integral values. The majority work hard to make ends meet, therefore efforts would be better spent ensuring wages meet the cost of living so that family time can be spent on individual values. By Republicans reigniting their confidence they are capable of rejecting association with those groups. That does, however, require support from everyone.

Some officials use Propaganda to ignite their agendas. For example, to insinuate that Democrats will "come to take your guns" and abolish the second amendment, and feed rhetoric to that effect is absurd, and negligent. We don't know that gun safety measures won't work because common sense legislation has never been enforced on a national level. The responsibility of leadership is to prevent unnecessary tragedy. The absolute refusal to improve the ACA, without an alternative program in place, speaks volumes to the people of this country on where the party stands on compromise.

Our nation can benefit from the Republicans commitment to real fiscal responsibility, traditional values, and reinvestment into the military. There is a desire from the people to see these assets in action. Republicans can offer these skills without absolutists in their way. When the Republican Party chooses people first, embraces compromise, and commits to alliance with multi-affiliation representation, then Republican officials can achieve these important goals.

▶ INDEPENDENTS

The Constitution does not bind us to a two-party-dominant system. People have come to believe that we have no other options and actually go to great lengths to ostracize those who do not "fall in line". This consolidation of power is skewed, and as a result, many constituents have unfortunately followed suit. Again, we recognize the divisiveness that flip-flopping brings.

When listening to people's perceptions of what Independents represent, one can conclude there is an "idea" that will never come to be. There seems to never be a good time to vote for an Independent because "there is always too much at stake for a lost vote". If the stakes are always too high, then it is fair to say the system isn't working. Interesting to discover if, and when, the country will decide it is a good time. Independent means to be unaffiliated to either party, but an Independent can stand for many different ideologies, and platforms. Some may stand for progress, and bridging the partisan gap while others lean toward Libertarian views that all should be on their own and programs paid for by the private sector. Other examples include Senator Bernie Sanders and President Donald Trump, who chose to run under a dominant party, but made it clear they do not truly identify as such. This in itself validates the importance of knowing who candidates are and not assume their stances based on their affiliation, or lack thereof.

Independents are *not* the same thing as a "dominant third party". They do not coalesce into one single platform. The very fact that they don't is the ultimate power of Independent voting. They are, in some capacity, our current system's "checks and balance", because they force major parties to include a greater populous and craft better bills.

Registering as Unaffiliated does not guarantee a vote for an Independent. In many cases unaffiliated voters will continue to vote party line. The original basis for the unaffiliated option was to represent the swing voter, the voter who will truly vote for their best candidate regardless of party. In both cases these are citizens who are fundamentally less attached to an affilia-tion but most likely still have strong ideologies. These are the citizens that are most likely to support multi-affiliation leadership, because they don't believe the answers lie in just one or the other party.

The biggest challenge for Independents is voter suppression and dominant party interference. Through awareness and action, a movement toward resolve will happen, but in the meantime, they must invest in continuity and what they exemplify. Clarity is more important today than ever, in order for the people to distinguish between the individual candidates and the many grassroots Independent parties. A candidate's stances are at the mercy of many points of view and inaccurate media spins. Explanations of what labels mean to each candidate would make a big difference in avoiding public assumptions.

The numbers of unaffiliated voters are rising. The United States has close to 42%, versus the Republicans and Democrats who split the remainder. If this percentage were to be a true reflection on actual votes for Independent candidates, then the fears of lost votes would be highly inaccurate.

As Independents evolve in confidence and conviction, they are capable of reaching the majority of unaffiliated voters. By supporting the best of both dominant parties, and creating innovative platforms of their own, Independents can become significant leaders. The potential of Independents shifting the dynamics of our dominant two-party system and pushing the dangerous extremes to the fringe is highly likely, if they do not also lose sight of their purpose.

— ★ —

Revitalizing hope in the majority's ability to affect change is crucial now. Both Parties are guilty of creating this devastating lack of trust for our politicians. Both parties participate in gerrymandering in order to secure their desired candidates. Both Parties undermine opportunity for Moderates and Independents to have a fair opportunity to run. Both parties have lost sight of how to truly work for the people and have allowed financial backers to dictate their accomplishments. The expectation of our elected officials is that they represent our collective voices, and utilize the strengths of their fellow civil servants. NEXT20 leaders do not undermine the execution of a policy they are not in agreement with, but ensures it is held to the highest standards and embodies what the experts have discovered. The leaders of the NEXT20 invite only experts into administration cabinets and understand the importance of our state representatives being accountable in producing unanimous support of solid policies in a timely manner. NEXT20 asks of the people to accept responsibility in due diligence of research and vote for the most integral candidates across the board. NEXT20 sets a new standard in which qualified candidates will become the leaders of the next twenty years and beyond.

STRATEGIES ☆

NEXT20 DOES NOT FALL VICTIM TO the fallacy and pressures of the partisan system. NEXT20 does not require changing affiliation; it requires maintaining dedication to leadership strengths, beliefs and values. If you consider yourself a Moderate or Independent, now is the time to own it. Do not just say it because you think that it qualifies as compromise or that it makes people feel safer: it does not. NEXT20 does not decrease strength and conviction but unifies it.

It begins in our communities. Leaders show conviction and willingness to compromise by listening to constituents of the opposing party and by standing together. Teams of multi-affiliation running mates utilize their individual expertise as strengths. When speaking to their communities as a unified force, and standing behind what each bring to the table, communities will then do the same. Leadership must simultaneously unite the voices in each town, city and county, and talk about the benefits of compromise. Gather in town halls, local parks, community centers and schools. Networks will spread the word. Media loves "surprises" and "different", so this is right in line. Show the people that working in partnership is in the best interest of our nation and will see justice through. These steps must begin now.

The coming generations require guidelines that make sense. The next generations don't identify with either of our dominant parties because they see the divide and want no part of the limitations. **NEXT20** is about them, their children and so on. The leaders of today are the ones who need to come together and work as a team so we can pass down an effective path to them.

Walking away from the establishments as they exist today is being true to our affiliations.

Walking away from the establishments as they exist today is being true to our affiliations. Those who refuse compromise are the disingenuous ones. The isolated representation of extremes is what damages a nation, but the combination of diverse expertise is what empowers.

There is no value in blame. All of us share the responsibility for where we are today. Instead of pointing fingers we need to solve problems. **NEXT20** sees the value in acknowledging accountability and can apologize for not compromising sooner. However, maintains a laser focus on the future and what is next to come. Remember how overwhelmed people are, how perceptions have been influenced, and how culture plays an integral role in our world. Our country can learn from the past and commit to more effective ways of inclusive leadership.

People of all income levels take advantage. The leaders of the NEXT20 do not target a specific group as the cause of our problems and ask of their constituents to follow suit. Some believe that those in poverty receiving federal assistance are "taking advantage." Others feel strongly that the wealthy receiving federal assistance filing for bankruptcies and foreclosures are the true "advantage takers." The leadership of the NEXT20 eliminates this division by focusing on reforms that reduce advantage taking across the board and secure the opportunities for those who truly need assistance.

The people of this nation deserve the bipartisan representation that they have believed in, hoped for and upon which they still wait.

The people of this nation deserve the collaborative representation that they have believed in, hoped for and upon which they still wait. There are many "liberal" citizens voting Republican, and many "conservatives" voting Democratic. The definitions vary person to person and state to state. It is not rational to expect 300 plus million diverse perspectives to be stuffed into two neat and tidy boxes.

Yes, constituents hold their representatives accountable to the platform on which they ran, and yes, those were delivered partially due to affiliation. NEXT20 concludes that neither party standing alone can accomplish those important goals.

Obligation to leadership is first and foremost, regardless of party representation. **NEXT20** gives our nation's people the credit they deserve in affirming what united leadership can accomplish.

The Leaders of the **NEXT20** are committed to:

- Reforming and improving our policies that enhance the lives of all.
- Embracing leadership partners from all affiliations—people who bring skills to the table that serve the needs of their communities.
- Representing bipartisan leadership in its true form by choosing country and its people over party.
- Seeking guidance of community leaders and professionals in order to be inclusive.
- Accepting funds that are solely in the interest of united goals.
- Guiding constituents interdependently.
- Ensuring our economy is stable by securing our Foundation.

As a result of these powerful actions being taken simultaneously across our nation, our leaders will be a part of something that has never before happened. The blended social and moral platforms of our leadership will be taken seriously through true conviction and compromise. These leaders, along with the support of the majority, will be the leaders who hold our nation together for the next twenty years and beyond.

CHOOSING
THE MAJORITY

OUR NATION IS MADE UP OF CONTRIBUTORS who make positive marks on our lives, every moment of every day. We share with many of these people affiliations in common. We also share our affiliations with those who do not represent us as individuals. Criminals of all kinds, racists, faith believers, non-believers, and opportunists exist among us. To insist that anyone is more righteous based on affiliation choice, is absurd and counter intuitive.

The burden of choice limits us and has fallen heavy on our leaders and our people. It is revealing how much we care. People in every corner of the country are identifying what is at stake and working hard to find answers. The only thing we are missing is the leadership that sets our bar higher and can unify us so that our efforts become worthy.

The people of our land are here for the same reasons, and that is because the United States represents freedom in opportunity and welcomes diversity. All people desire opportunity, a safe nation, and a strong economy. These are common threads that hold us together. Our future leadership must embrace commonality, in order to succeed.

Our most influential leaders are already lining up their partisan strategies. Partisanship thrives on the weakness of the opposing party to be the ticket to their success, and media exploiters irresponsibly profit off our divide. Once again, we settle. The formula NEXT20 also acknowledges those who won't vote for settling and those who can't vote due to oppression. Now is the time to accept the fact that the voices of the majority are not represented, and every time we are forced to choose we lose the opportunity to become the strong, healthy nation of which we are capable. NEXT20 ensures our story will not end because we lack the creativity to unite. NEXT20 has to begin now.

The people of our country desire freedom from dangerous absolutism and self-destruction. We reject those who divide us and take advantage of our vulnerability. We desire the opportunity to combat oppression through unified leadership. We desire a chance to experience the benefits of choosing compromise. We desire a country that stands for integrity.

Now is the time, while the evidence of need is profound, to create a more perfect union.

FOUNDATIONS ☆

THE NEXT20 REFERS TO THE MOST VITAL support systems as our "foundations." These are six interdependent examples that are all currently neglected. When basic support systems are nurtured with consistent attention our country will no longer be forced to debate the purpose of these foundations. After all, the partisan flip-flopping only produces extreme amounts of waste and economic insecurity. Health care, Education, Immigration, National Security, Environment and Opportunity are interdependent, and our country's economic security depends on them in a highly functioning state. The following pages explain how each contribute and why they must be protected.

Through the bold actions of our NEXT20 leaders, the next generation will be handed solid foundations with responsibility to uphold them, without the burden of reinventing failed systems they did not create.

▷ HEALTH CARE

During the 1960s our political ideologies were tested and major shifts in leadership platforms challenged us. It was President Lyndon B. Johnson, representing the Conservative Democrats at the time, who took on the controversial "War on Poverty." Regardless of the division in our country before and after the assassination of John F. Kennedy, our government was able, through bipartisan leadership and compromise, to provide the baseline for the Medicaid and Medicare programs we have today. These programs offered an initial infusion into our economy and have provided support to our citizens for decades.

Our current problems lie in the lack of attention to reforming nationwide health care. NEXT20 does not question the purpose of these health care programs, but rather offers solutions on how to make them beneficial today and into the future.

Our current system only guarantees affordable quality coverage for those who work for a company that provides and subsidizes health care plans. This has created a distorted view of entitlement and disparity in financial security. Misconceptions that one person is better than another based solely on the job they hold are detrimental. The self-employed, skilled laborers, small business owners and divorcees are just as vital to our economy as a president of a company, the corporate employee, and the attorney, etc., and are entitled to equal health care opportunities. A system where all have access to the same plans, regardless of career choice, reduces disparity and revitalizes our economy.

When all are provided health care benefits, it opens doors economically, allowing individuals to choose career paths and business ventures freely. This not only relieves stress, which results in better job performance, but also creates an economic boost. The boost in turn enables employers to have the funds to provide salary increases, bonus programs and increase company resources. Work environment standards would improve due to the positive pressure of broader competition. It is a win-win for everyone.

Utilizing the protective aspects of our current Affordable Care Act (ACA) in combination with the most valuable private insurance benefits is important. All potential risks must be considered regardless of what the programs are named. Single Payer Plan is conceptually an efficient avenue if the government structures are willing to support reform. Universal Care suggests a collaboration of the various approaches. In a few states private insurers have been incentivized to offer lower cost plans that fill the gaps of the uninsured. NEXT20 doesn't focus on what it is called, it focuses on what works. As long as all people have access to quality affordable care, and the health care facilities can afford to prosper, the effort is a success. Pre-existing conditions, preventative care, mental health care and low deductibles are possible when all are given the opportunity to participate. Pharmaceuticals, medical products, and insurance companies will be held accountable to a standard of reasonable profit margins. Hospitals and health care professionals will have to accommodate yet another adjustment but they will be included in the process of building a more efficient system.

Funding from private donors will go toward hospital improvements instead of covering the costs of the uninsured. Establishing higher quality care is achievable when the number of participants increases and the profit margins decrease. Creating a market for insurance companies to gain from incentives in not-for-profit status is also considered under NEXT20. If suppliers of these health care services and products refuse to adjust their profits and comply with policies for the greater good, they will not be chosen to participate in the health care programs.

In order to match today's cost of living, premiums should fall between $75 and $500 per month; never exceeding $500 per month per family regardless of income, unless one chooses a higher premium for a deluxe coverage package. Premiums are way out of balance with the current cost of living. The money people will save on insurance premiums will return back into our economy. People can then save to purchase homes, own their own business, invest in the stock market, fund activities, fund education, choose healthier lifestyles, and become more self-sufficient. This results in a thriving economy and lifts weight off of government spending. NEXT20 understands that by offering equal access to health care, livelihoods would increase, and desperation would diminish. Capitalism can flourish with a solid healthcare foundation.

Medicaid

When health care premiums reduce, the number of people who rely on Medicaid will reduce. When the ability to participate in a health care program is no longer a daunting task, people will be incentivized if possible to achieve higher incomes. This will relieve government expenses and allow for those funds to transfer to other areas, like the elderly and disabled. With this reform, there will be an expansion in the network of doctors who accept Medicaid and an improvement in the fair use opportunities for those on it.

Medicaid, like welfare, serves an important purpose. The key to success with these support systems is in ensuring that the leap into less dependency is an attainable goal. NEXT20 understands the reality of the current cost of living, health care expenses and how unreasonable the expectations are of the general population. NEXT20 emphasizes that health care must be an equal opportunity system, with room for adjustments that are determined by the variables of each state, and that compliance and state regulations must be equal.

Women's Health

Women make up 51% of the U.S. population. This means that in order to maintain a strong and stable economy, which is the goal of all governing platforms, women must be able to family plan, care for their health and their families, and successfully participate in our nation's workforce. Women's health care is undeniably the most important aspect of economic growth and our ability to prioritize family values.

Historically speaking, women's health has always been a bipartisan priority. The importance of expanding federal funding to reduce poverty through Medicaid had already begun. In the

1970s, the expansion continued under President Nixon's administration. The Senate and the House voted in overwhelming support of Title X. Title X specifically protects care services for family planning and preventative health, for those otherwise without it. These efforts not only recognized that providing health care was essential to lift people out of poverty, but it opened our eyes to the bipartisan conclusion that women's health is vital to our nation's growth and stability. NEXT20 commits to maintaining equal access to health care for women of all socioeconomic backgrounds, regardless from which provider it comes.

In 1973, the U.S. Supreme Court, wherein five out of seven Supreme Court Justices were nominated by Republican Presidents, ruled in favor of the federal freedom of choice. Their decision was based on the facts presented as to why choice is justified and essential in ensuring women can make safe choices for themselves. This decision was not in connection with any restrictions associated with women's access to health care.

Under President Jimmy Carter, a Democrat, the Hyde Amendment was passed. This was an amendment that separated the federal funding of women's health and eliminated all funding of abortion. It was a conservative measure to accommodate the anti-choice movement and eliminate funds that supported a highly controversial topic. Unfortunately, the only women impacted by the Hyde Amendment are the women with the lowest socioeconomic status. Freedom of choice continued for those privately insured and able to pay, without impact on their access to health care. Since then, private donations have reduced the gap of funding necessary to provide freedom of choice to less fortunate women, making the law in effect fair to women of all incomes. Federal spending for abortion services has already been eradicated, through the Hyde Agreement.

The platform of our current administration targets women's health care provided by the federal government through Medicaid. Proposing bills that defund all organizations associated with providing abortions targets not only the health of the uninsured, but the health of every woman on Medicaid. As a result, by targeting organizations, all care is eliminated. Title X is in place to ensure that preventative health care funding remains available to those who are uninsured and on Medicaid. It is not only unethical to dismantle Title X, but unconstitutional to target any specific organization or class of people. There are laws in our constitution to protect us from this form of government, and those laws must be upheld.

Under the leadership of the NEXT20, ongoing debates on isolated topics will never interfere with access to health care for anyone.

PUBLIC EDUCATION

Public Education has always been and will always be a bipartisan foundation. Public schools must be able to offer the vast array of learning options 21st century students require. Consistent attention to reform is necessary. Standardized testing, if inconclusive, can take away from curriculum-focused time and strangle a student's ability to effectively learn. Testing can provide baseline information, but cannot replace the value of learning time, or meet the needs of the diverse styles of how kids learn. Thus, it is imperative that regulation and oversight of school environments is in place to ensure that high standards are upheld, but also allow teachers and learning specialists the freedom to enhance learning through creativity. By cutting costs due to unnecessary testing and re-evaluating expenses in top-heavy administrations, funds would then be available for teacher pay increases and extracurricular activities. Students would become exposed to and have the choice of creative outlets, athletics and trade skills. All students, regardless of socioeconomic diversity, should have the opportunity to attend schools that offer them adequate support systems. Accommodations for learning differences must be a national priority in today's world.

Our teachers' ability to personally thrive in the communities where they teach is essential in creating successful school communities. A typical teacher takes on several roles. They are coaches, tutors, support systems and maintain required education of their own. They are responsible for every aspect of our children's time with them, and salaries should reflect the importance of their roles. Considerations like forgiven percentage of home loan interest can also be considered to ensure they are compensated for their dedication.

The broader the access to outlets students have in their areas of interest, the more successful they can become. Non-compete after school sports and performing arts in addition to competitive clubs, must be available in order for all students to tap into their potential talents. School activity sharing and parent involvement can contribute to providing these activities. The success of these opportunities, will lead to an overall reduction in bullying, drug use, depression and teen suicide. When there is a balance of attention given to activities and support, rather than just to standards and regulations, we will see improvement in education overall.

Graduates today learn to teach to the needs of all students and have the skills to navigate the needs of their generation. The NEXT20 seeks guidance from university teaching programs to assist in structuring the priorities in K-12 programs, and the leaders of the NEXT20 commit to seeing that these resources are utilized.

School of Choice
It is important to support all opportunities for a variety of learning environments. School choice is essential.

Vouchers
NEXT20 holds firm that in order for schools to receive federal funding they must be equally accountable to regulation. It is reasonable to consider future allocation of federal funds distributed differently, only if the schools are structured in ways that offer equal opportunity.

Public Education is supported by all affiliations. The Department of Education must maintain leadership that represents all socioeconomic income levels, bipartisanship and most importantly, every child. **NEXT20** understands the gravity of importance of this foundation for the future and the economy.

▶ IMMIGRATION

The U.S. has always been a safe haven for immigrants and refugees. Immigration reform is needed and should be a joint, compromise effort between the Administration and Congress. It is imperative that we maintain precautionary measures. Opportunity to populations must be fair and inclusive and reflect the diverse population of the United States.

Refugees and Those Seeking Asylum

For the most vulnerable, refugees and those requesting asylum, our vetting process is among the most rigorous of Western countries as is. There is no reason to delay their admittance due to country of origin or religion. If there is a need for delay, it should be based only on readiness of the U.S. to provide adequately for their well-being. Congress and the Administration should continue the tradition of fairness for those forced to leave their countries where, many times, there is U.S. involvement in the conflict.

Immigrants Applying for Legal Entry

For those immigrants applying for legal entry, visa reform is needed to speed up the long waits. The Australian merit-based points system could be a model for the U.S. in order to ensure immigrants who come here for education and skilled labor jobs find a more secure path to career opportunities. That would also increase the guarantee that American-born students have a fair chance as they seek education and job security. Exclusivity to the most educated applicants would be a detrimental in balance of opportunity for the qualified citizens born here who have already invested in their expertise. Naturalization should be promoted to encourage full participation in life in the U.S.

Undocumented Immigrants

Undocumented immigrants present the need for the greatest system reform. Faster sentencing for crimes and immediate evaluation if deportation is warranted and would alleviate the need for more detention centers. There should be protection against deportation and a path to legalization for those brought here as children. Only under the circumstances of criminal charges should a child ever be separated from their families. Action should be taken to enforce penalties against employers who abuse illegal immigrants. Employers should be required to use the e-verify program to make sure new hires are legal. Undocumented immigrants working in agriculture and tourism must be legalized. Legalize those who have passed a background check and pay a reasonable fine. The Pew Research Center's Fact Tank reports that the apprehension of Mexicans at the U.S. border has dropped to the lowest levels in fifty years. We can use resources toward policies and programs that would create a reformed immigration system instead of the high costs of a border wall and additional detention centers, resources that would have a positive impact on economic growth for all.

When redefining border security, the careful measures above reduce potential traumatic results of which immigrants are at risk. NEXT20 prioritizes the security of our nation and accepts responsibility for the safety of our immigrants.

▶ NATIONAL SECURITY

National security is a major role of Congress and the president requires cooperation and compromise to ensure the survival and security of our nation. Not only does it affect our foreign policy and defense but impacts our economy, monetary policies, and natural resources. That role has been in existence since the establishment of the constitution and will continue for at least the next twenty years.

Our first line of defense of national security should be diplomacy. Too many American lives have been spent on actions that promote and satisfy our need to be a world power. The need for bipartisan cooperation of the parties in congress is self-evident. Compromise, regardless of political philosophy is the only way the concept of global allies and national security can be realized.

In order to establish those policies, the intelligence community must provide the informational base for our foreign policy as events occur throughout the world. It is imperative that the intelligence community be focused on the primary goal of support to the decision makers.

Senate and House intelligence committees are charged with oversight for the intelligence community. In the next twenty years Congress should involve itself more in the oversight of the intelligence community to ensure protection of the American people under increased threat possibilities. That oversight should involve monitoring the functions of the intelligence community with close budget review and planning. Budget priorities dictate oversight roles that prevent duplication within the intelligence community while ensuring timely intelligence.

Multi-affiliation compromise would result in more efficient border security policies to avoid the high costs of a wall between the U.S. and Mexico. This would more effectively ensure the security of both borders. NEXT20 leaders are committed to protecting the United States from the potential threats of our times. With this also comes the assurance that the Administration will choose carefully our involvement in foreign lands and nevermore use harmful methods of provocation. The emphasis on expenditures for the re-institution of aggressive Cold War defense strategies instead could be directed to other national security programs. Those programs could include funding to provide comparable rigorous training to reservists to be able to effectively replace regular military. Funds could also be used for new technology, especially to address threats in cyberspace.

National Security within our borders also requires the United States gun laws and registries are as accurate as possible. NEXT20 confirms the security of the Second Amendment and also establishes noninvasive national stays and protocols that minimize to the best of ability, acts of violence due to domestic terrorists and mental health issues. Nonpartisan committees made up of long standing gun owners, teachers, students and mental health providers must be included in the decision making. Putting into place efficient non-invasive gun safety measures, is imperative for our nation's security.

Our strengthened economy through the foundations of NEXT20 are a big step toward achieving a Democracy that cannot easily be threatened. Protecting our military must come with asking them to protect us. Their service deserves our utmost attention. Ongoing reinvestments in their training, when abroad, and their lives after they return home, is vital to our national security.

▶ ENVIRONMENT

NEXT20 understands that we must not have to *believe* climate change exists, in order to make the care of our planet a priority. The health of the environment is equally as important to our personal health and our economy; in fact, they are completely intertwined. Without clean air and soil, our immune systems are compromised, and our resources diminish.

This is again a foundation that requires multi-affiliation leadership in order to invest in discovering the best solutions. Solar energy, wind energy, reductions in fossil fuels, and waste management are all on the table. The leaders of the NEXT20 are committed to utilizing and implementing all resources available that participate in long-term environmental health.

On April 22, 2016 the United States committed to the world-wide efforts to minimize the damage to our environment. The United States ranks in the top three countries that contribute to the pollution in the atmosphere. Our atmosphere is what protects us from global warming. With a damaged ozone layer, temperatures continue to rise. Our nation is responsible for reducing our carbon emissions, such as coal, oil and natural gas. Deforestation, soil erosion and animal agriculture also play a huge role in the damage to which we contribute. At our current rate, the result of global warming will be in an acute state by the year 2047. Our country must commit to the reduction of global warming, taking every step recommended by experts to work diligently toward a sustainable future.

The aim under the Paris Agreement reads as such:

"(a) Holding the increase in the global average temperature to well below 2˚C above pre-industrial levels and to pursue efforts to limit the temperature increase to 1.5˚C above pre-industrial levels, recognizing that this would signifi-cantly reduce the risks and impacts of climate change;

(b) Increasing the ability to adapt to the adverse impacts of climate change and foster climate resilience and low greenhouse gas emissions development, in a manner that does not threaten food production;

Making finance flows consistent with a pathway towards low greenhouse gas emissions and climate-resilient development.

The regulations around food sources also need reform. There are strides being taken but only with national support can this be done. The harmful methods still used in some agriculture and factory farming productions is putting our citizens' health at risk. Farming that continues to use mistreatment of workers, animals and methods that are absolute must be accountable to highest of standards. Prioritizing that our precious water is clean and lead amounts are reduced, is at the top of the list. All of these factors ultimately impact the health of all people.

We should not ignore the men and women in our workforce that struggle during industry transitions. Through continuous forward thinking, we can include support for our workers as we define the shifts in our investments. With federal funding and the contributions from all industries, the heavy burdens on our workers and our economy can be lifted.

Everyone must participate in caring for our environment for us to see the benefits of our efforts. It is only a matter of shifting how we operate. Through an infusion of information throughout our communities as well as focused efforts, our country can achieve this shift. The Atlanta airport is a great example of how cities are taking steps by providing trash compactors, recycling bins and filtered water taps. Increased availability of recycling methods for businesses and communities is a priority under the leadership of the NEXT20. The expectation must be that the people of the United States raise their respect level for life in general. How we treat the environment and animals is a direct reflection on how we treat each other. Protection of animals, domestic, wild and food sourced deserve to be protected from neglect and abuse. This is the easiest of our problems to solve.

In no other industry has innovation been halted due to the financial "hit" companies may endure, the way it has been in relationship to our environment. Consulting and investing in technology and energy experts is essential now, more than it ever was in the past.

Following in the footsteps of cities and states globally, we can achieve the goals we committed to as stated in the Paris agreement. NEXT20 takes global leadership seriously and strives for the United States to be amongst the most progressive countries on behalf of long-term environmental sustainability.

▷ SAFETY AND OPPORTUNITY

NEXT20 takes into consideration the long history of challenges our country has faced in ensuring that all people are safe and have opportunity in our nation. There are endless reasons why there will always be people suffering, left behind and over-looked. It is also true that there will always be some people, due to their prejudices, threatened by others' access to opportunity. This is an unfortunate aspect of humanity, but it is even more unfortunate that it is enabled by not prioritizing efforts to resolve it. First, we all must participate in deflecting the notion that only *some* people benefit from a renewed investment. Second, we must make every effort to minimize the number of people trapped in these dire scenarios. Implementing the foundations of **NEXT20** will certainly help in moving toward fair opportunity, but we will still have a lot of work to do.

We are all impacted by this. Not only should it weigh on our conscience, it has tremendous impacts on our economy. Our country has the resources to provide every community in our country with access to education and employment. We have the resources to give our youth incentives to avoid a path of crime, and a road to education. We can share our cities without detrimental displacement of any citizens. Our criminal justice systems can be held to ethical standards, and we can build systems based on prevention. Through leadership that represents and supports our majority goals, opportunities can exist for all.

It is hard to grasp that today; our partisan systems are still creating serious levels of disparity. Under the state of our current Administration, and the divisiveness of the people, the gap continues to grow. Labor workers all across America are still working in abusive and substandard conditions. For the same petty crimes, some teenagers are left in harsh prisons, while others receive community service and a fine. Trafficking rings are somehow not able to be found, but we find resources to fund ICE in the deportation of nonviolent, undocumented immigrants. Native Americans must continue to protect their land, and we still continue the debate of LGBTQIA equal rights. Our poor children need support, and the costs for our seniors are too high. Our homeless face dehumanization and the Foster Care system can barely sustain. The racial tensions between police and citizens are also the result of partisan government neglect.

Though we are faced with more problems than mentioned here, we must reinvest in our fight for justice, but this time no one gets left behind. Our government wastes millions on campaigns, political bureaucracy and irresponsible choices—resources that could and should be made available to solve society's ills. Individuals will perceive the implementation of these foundations as beneficial to only some. It is the responsibility of leadership and the support of the majority, to commit for the long haul, and prove the benefits for all.

The safety and opportunity of all citizens also includes a responsibility to contribute on behalf of our country. This expectation is contingent upon establishing a national voter system that leaves us with certainty its validity. NEXT20 leadership stands behind one national voting system with the same standards in each state, because every voice must be recognized. After all, elections are supposed to be a reflection of every electorate in the nation.

There is a reason our forefathers had the wisdom to structure the Constitution the way they did. "All Men are Equal" and the "Separation of Church and State" were specifically designed, based on prior history, to protect our country's future. Capitalism is not threatened by broadening opportunity; in fact, the better off every individual is, the wealthier our nation becomes.

Not all of us are competing for super wealth. For the majority, wealth is defined as the freedom to not have to live paycheck to paycheck, and to have the ability to offer ourselves and our children opportunities. Quality of life and room to devote to our values are precious, and no one should be denied these. NEXT20 understands that safety and opportunity are key in everyone's ability to succeed.

— ★ —

These interdependent foundations examine how the basic necessities of a strong nation are achieved. Democracy includes capitalistic opportunity with social support systems. Only with both can the United States live up to what it stands for. They must be secured and non-negotiable regardless of elected officials. Investment and improvements due to ever-changing needs is the only goal in order for any formula to be viable. Candidates would then be chosen based on expertise and leadership qualities rather than dismantlement, and consequently resources would be revived. There is no country that has a flawless system, and there are many examples of pros and cons to follow. We must consider the size of our nation, the resources in our nation and define our best possible solutions for our time. NEXT20 is a simple formula, it requires is a reset in the way we approach our goals and takes advantage of the best in who we are.

IN CLOSING . . . ☆

IN THIS VERY MOMENT, there exists a unique opportunity to unite the vast concerns of the people. Renewed faith in multi-affiliation accomplishments and realization of the American dream are obtainable with leadership committed to stability. Now that the awareness level is prevalent, there is no reason to waste precious time revolving an inefficient partisan cycle ever again. Now is the time to attend to progress for the next twenty years. Now is the time to move beyond the stagnancy of today and leave our next generations with the foundations that will ensure their ability to thrive.

It is undeniable that the people of this country asked for change. Future leaders must trust that the desire for a more perfect union exists, and the people are ready and waiting. Now is the time for those leaders to show us who they are, so that the people can stand together with them. Now is the time, while the door to change is open, for leaders to direct our country with integrity, and move the dangerous extremes to the fringe where they belong.

Shortly after the November 2016 election, I chose to reach out to my community in hopes to find others with similar concerns. I hosted a gathering at my home where six strangers arrived. To my surprise, it was discovered that all affiliations were represented among us. This is where NEXT20 began.

The NEXT20 formula unites tradition, maintains ideology, promotes progress, and combines the best of all affiliations. NEXT20 takes tradition into the 21st century.

If these pages inspire you to support leadership that exemplifies progress through commonality and compromise, then NEXT20 accomplishes its goal. There are many people and organizations sharing messages in line with NEXT20. Let us join together and create a movement that makes our awareness purposeful. We invite you to join in further exploration of the strengths of multi-affiliation leadership and secured foundations at www.NEXT20now.com.

NEXT20

REFERENCES

http://www.policyinnovations.org/ideas/commentary/data/000002

https://www.google.com/amp/s/thinkprogress.org/amp/p/7b9b3893c9de?
client=safari

https://prod-static-ngop-pbl.s3.amazonaws.com/docs/2012GOPPlatform.pdf

http://www.femalista.com/
george-w-bushs-daughter-will-headline-planned-parenthood-fundraiser/

http://m.huffpost.com/us/entry/us_58a77e73e4b026a89a7a2b08

http://news.wgbh.org/2017/03/15/politics-government/
major-new-study-shows-political-polarization-mainly-right-wing

http://awm.com/ohio-passes-law-that-makes-any-form-of-animal-abuse-a-
felony-charge-do-you-support-this-4/?utm_medium=facebook&utm_
source=nsp&utm_content=20170317_1000

https://thethoughtfulcoalminer.com/

http://www.economist.com/news/united-states/21616962-neel-kashkari-will-not-
unseat-californias-democratic-governor-he-may-help-his-party

http://www.jsonline.com/story/news/blogs/wisconsin-voter/2017/04/15/
donald-trumps-election-flips-both-parties-views-economy/100502848/

http://m.huffpost.com/us/entry/us_564de8c2e4b031745cf0026f

https://www.carnegiecouncil.org/publications/archive/policy_innovations

http://www.nydailynews.com/news/national/
king-african-americans-won-trusting-broken-justice-system-article-1.3179495

https://bipartisanpolicy.org/

https://www.census.gov/topics

https://en.wikipedia.org/wiki/Paris_Agreement

http://www.pewresearch.org/

www.epa.gov

www.onegreenplanet.org

https://investinginkids.net

http://educationnext.org/key-innovation-regulation/

housingmattersupdate@urban.org

https://www.guttmacher.org

https://www.nas.org/

https://en.wikipedia.org/wiki/The_Capitalist_Manifesto

https://bipartisanpolicy.org/library/a-bipartisan-approach-to-americas-fiscal-future/

ACKNOWLEDGMENTS

Thank you to these contributors of **NEXT20** and all of those who offered support along the way.

Swede Grooms, Wanda and Robert Carlyle, Mira Meyer-Oertel, Hansen Longfellow, Angelin Thompson, Deb Hoople, Valerie Wadel, Christine Meyer-Oertel, Brian Douglas, Linda Jackson, Cheryl Chiasson, and Paul Dube.

Editor: Susan Claridge, Global Publishing Group LLC
Editor: Kirsten Jensen, My Word Publishing
Book design: Factor E Creative, Inc.
NEXT20 logo: Brian Roundtree
Publishing Consultant: Susie Schaefer, My Word Publishing

ABOUT THE AUTHOR

CLAUDIA JAMES is a first generation American. She has been influenced by her European immigrant parents and her life's exposure to cultural diversity. Claudia is passionate about sharing her vision for our future leadership, and the responsibility which comes by uniting the common threads of our multi-cultural citizens. Claudia lives in Denver, Colorado and enjoys life with her family of seven, including their dogs Duke and Eva.

NOTES

NOTES